WACKY WORLD OF... STRANGE SCIENCE!

by
Hermione Redshaw

BEARPORT
PUBLISHING

Minneapolis, Minnesota

CREDITS

All images are courtesy of Shutterstock.com, unless otherwise specified. With thanks to Getty Images, Thinkstock Photo, and iStockphoto.

Recurring assets – Lelene (header font), MaryMB (explosion), RoyaltyFreeStockVectors (spiral), Ardea, hvostik (series logo), Amy Li (additional illustrations). Cover – Axel Bueckert, Hafiez Razali, p2–3 – wavebreakmedia, p4–5 – Helmut Fig Newton, Vladimir Sazonov, Skydive Erick, aureapterus, princessdlaf, p6–7 – FG Trade, p8–9 – Roman Samborskyi, Sergey Bezgodov, p10–11 – kwanchaichaiudom, gelpi, PedroMatos, TashaNatasha, p12–13 – Ian Sutton (wiki commons), p14–15 – Art_Photo, thekopmylife, p16–17 – Bobica10, chrisbrignell, GogaTao, Simon Kadula, p18–19 – Alyona Naive Angel, Alanstix64, p20–21 – it:lithiumclou, TashaNatasha, Alyona Naive Angel, Alanstix64, busypix, p22–23 – Belovodchenko Anton, Creativa Images, Lebid Volodymyr, Yulia_Bogomolova.

Library of Congress Cataloging-in-Publication Data is available at www.loc.gov or upon request from the publisher.

ISBN: 979-8-88509-383-5 (hardcover)
ISBN: 979-8-88509-505-1 (paperback)
ISBN: 979-8-88509-620-1 (ebook)

© 2023 Booklife Publishing
This edition is published by arrangement with Booklife Publishing.

North American adaptations © 2023 Bearport Publishing Company. All rights reserved. No part of this publication may be reproduced in whole or in part, stored in any retrieval system, or transmitted in any form or by any means, electronic, mechanical, photocopying, recording, or otherwise, without written permission from the publisher.

For more information, write to Bearport Publishing, 5357 Penn Avenue South, Minneapolis, MN 55419.

CONTENTS

SCIENCE 4

A YEAR IN BED 6

MAKING A MEMORY 8

MEMORY TEST 10

REAL-LIFE ZOMBIES 12

TURNING WATER TO GOLD? 14

GLITTER-PROOF WATER 16

HUMAN-MADE VOLCANO 18

HOMEMADE ERUPTION 20

SLIGHTLY STRANGE 22

GLOSSARY 24

INDEX 24

SCIENCE

There is no doubt that humans do some very strange things. We make lobster telephone art and turn old milk into clothing. We **design** wacky, twisty buildings and more.

Science explains some of the strangest things in our world. Whether smart, silly, or downright strange, scientists will never stop trying to learn about the many mysteries of our world.

A YEAR IN BED

Humans have long looked to the stars with questions. Some wondered what would happen to **astronauts'** bodies in space. To find out, scientists decided to get into bed!

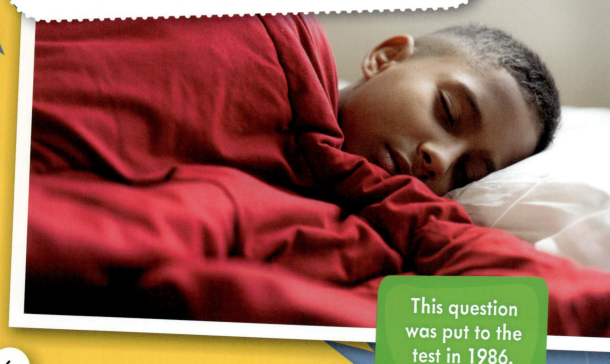

This question was put to the test in 1986.

Scientists studied people who spent a year lying down. The **participants** could not leave their beds for anything, even to use the toilet. They had helpers who would bring them everything they needed.

After a year in bed, the earthbound astronauts had to relearn sitting and walking.

MAKING A MEMORY

If you think that's odd, just imagine thinking about *thinking*. In 2012, scientists gave a mouse a fake memory of receiving a shock. This never really happened, but the mouse showed fear of being shocked again.

Many say this study by scientists Xu Liu and Steve Ramirez is helpful for understanding how memories are made. Someday, we might be able to help people who have lost their memories.

Xu Liu and Steve Ramirez later tried to give animals happy memories.

MEMORY TEST

Why not try your own memory **experiment** with friends. First, make a list of 10 nouns.

PART I: Read out the list of words for your friends to remember. Wait a minute, then have them repeat back the words.

Brother

Pumpkin

Tree

Gorilla

YOUR WORDS DO NOT NEED TO MAKE SENSE TOGETHER.

PART 2: Read out a list of 10 new words to your friends. This time, let them draw things about the words for a minute. When time is up, ask them to repeat the words back to you.

Did drawing help your friends remember more?

REAL-LIFE ZOMBIES

Some scientists are going beyond the brain. What can we do with the whole body? How about bring it back to life?! Scientists found small animals that had been frozen in ice for more than 20,000 years. And they brought them back to life!

The real-life zombies of this study were tiny living things called wheel animals.

Modern scientists are not the first people to try and **preserve** living things. People have been doing it for thousands of years in many different ways.

Ancient Egyptians wrapped their dead up as mummies to protect the bodies.

TURNING WATER TO GOLD?

Scientists have unlocked many secrets. Unfortunately, they still haven't discovered the secret to making gold. But they came close! They turned water into something that looked very similar to the real thing.

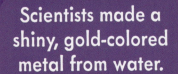

Scientists made a shiny, gold-colored metal from water.

Water is a liquid, and gold is a solid. You can make water into a solid by freezing it. However, it is much harder to turn water into something else entirely. Before this experiment, scientists didn't even think it was possible!

GLITTER-PROOF WATER

Scientists worked hard to turn water into a gold metal. But you can easily keep gold glitter out of water at home. First, sprinkle some glitter into a shallow pan of water. Then, grab some dish soap.

THIS EXPERIMENT ALSO WORKS WITH COCOA POWDER INSTEAD OF GLITTER.

Add a blob of dish soap to the middle of the water. Watch the glitter move away from the soap toward the edges of the dish.

17

HUMAN-MADE VOLCANO

Volcanoes can be scary and dangerous, but some scientists want to set one off... sort of! They think a volcanic **eruption** could help stop **global warming**.

GLOBAL WARMING IS WHEN EARTH GETS HOTTER BECAUSE OF HUMAN ACTIONS.

Instead of a real volcano, scientists would use a balloon high in the air to spray tiny bits of chalk across the ground. The idea is that the chalk would **reflect** the sun's light back into space and help the planet cool down.

A volcano actually cooled down parts of the Phillippines after it erupted in 1991.

HOMEMADE ERUPTION

You can create a small erupting volcano, too. First, gather your supplies:

- Baking soda
- Vinegar
- Red or orange food coloring
- An empty plastic bottle
- A funnel
- A tray or shallow dish

If you want, you can decorate the outside of your volcano.

Time to make your volcano!

1. Place the bottle in the tray or shallow dish.

2. Use a funnel to put some baking soda into the bottle.

3. Mix some food coloring and vinegar together.

4. Pour your mix into the bottle and stand back for the eruption!

SLIGHTLY STRANGE

Check out more silly science!

A HUNT FOR THE LOCH NESS MONSTER
- In 2018
- Scientists took water from Loch Ness to look for proof of a monster in the Scottish lake.

UN-BOILED EGG
- In 2015
- Scientists figured out how to unboil a boiled egg.

BEE STINGS
- In 2012
- A man let bees sting him to find out where stings hurt the most.

Even the most strange-sounding science tells us something about ourselves and the world. What will you find out? Anything is possible.

GLOSSARY

astronauts people who travel to space

design to think up, plan, or create

eruption the sending out of lava, ash, steam, and gas from a volcano

experiment a scientific test

global warming a rise in temperatures around the world

participants people who take part in something, such as an experiment

preserve to keep something safe and stop it from changing

reflect to bounce back light, heat, or sound

INDEX

bed 6–7

glitter 16–17

gold 14, 16–17

memory 8–10

mouse 8

mummies 13

preserve 13

volcano 18–21

zombie 12